KALEIDOSCOPE

BONES
AND
MUSCLES

by
Suzanne LeVert

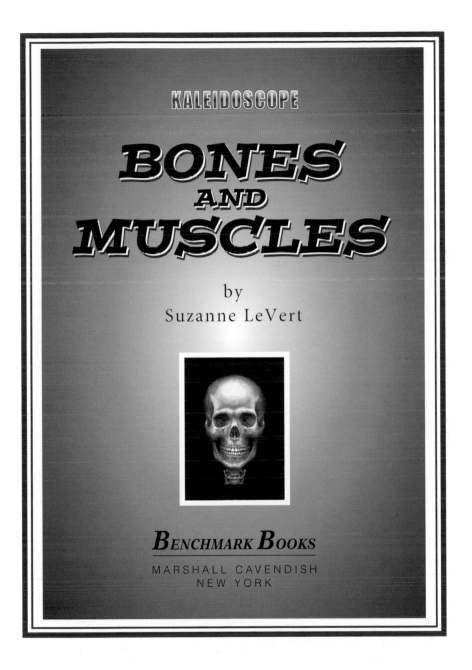

BENCHMARK **B**OOKS

MARSHALL CAVENDISH
NEW YORK

Benchmark Books
Marshall Cavendish Corporation
99 White Plains Road
Tarrytown, NY 10591-9001
Website: www.marshallcavendish.com

Library of Congress Cataloging-in-Publication Data

LeVert, Suzanne.
Bones and muscles / by Suzanne LeVert.
   p.cm. – (Kaleidoscope)
Includes bibliographical references and index.
ISBN 0-7614-1309-X
1. Musculoskeletal system—Juvenile literature. [1. Skeleton. 2. Bones. 3. Muscles.] I. Title. II. Series.
QP301 .L615 2001   612.7—dc21   00-050715

Photo Research by Anne Burns Images

Cover photo by Alex Grey, Peter Arnold, Inc.

Photos in this book are used by permission and through the courtesy of: *PhotoEdit:* David Young-Wolff, 5.
Phototake: CNRI, 6, 34; Siri Mills, 9, 33; John Karapelou, CMI, 29; ISM, 37; Barts Medical Library, 38 (upper and lower);
Teri McDermott, 41. *Photo Researchers:* Science Photo Libaray/Prof. P. Motta, 10; Astrid & Hanns-Frieder Michler, 13;
Mhau Kulyk, 22: Jean-Loup Charmet, 30; Michael Abbey/Science Source, 17. *Peter Arnold:* A. & F. Michler, 14, 21;
Alex Grey, 18, 25; SIU, 26; Bruce Curtis, 42.

Printed in Italy

6 5 4 3 2 1

CONTENTS

THE MOVERS AND SHAKERS   4

DEM BONES, DEM BONES   7

INSIDE YOUR BONES   11

BONES FROM HEAD TO TOE   15

MOVING WITH MUSCLES   24

HOW MUSCLES WORK   28

MUSCLES FROM HEAD TO TOE   31

WHEN THINGS GO WRONG   35

KEEPING YOUR BONES AND MUSCLES HEALTHY   43

GLOSSARY   44

FIND OUT MORE   46

INDEX   48

THE MOVERS AND SHAKERS

Stand still in front of a mirror and look at your body. Notice the shape of your head, the slant of your shoulders, the size of your feet. The bones that make up your skeleton give your body its form. Now move: Turn your head, make a fist, or jump up and down. You can do this because of the way your muscles and bones work together. Let's take a look inside and see how all this works.

This boy is flexing his biceps, one of the muscles that control the movement of the arm.

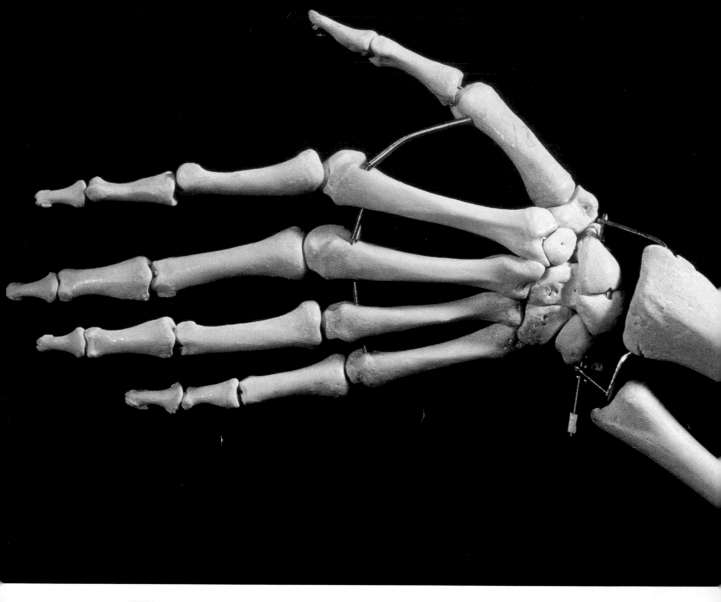

Although the bones in this skeleton are dead, the ones inside your body are very much alive.

DEM BONES, DEM BONES

If you look at a skeleton in your doctor's office or at school, you'll see that dead bones look pretty dried up and sticklike. The bones in your body, however, are teeming with life. Bones are living tissues that grow and develop as you get older until they've become the right size to give your body the shape and support it needs.

You were born with about 270 soft bones, but by the time you reach the age of twenty or twenty-five, you'll have about 206 hard, permanent bones. Many of your bones fuse together as you get older. Two hundred and six sounds like a lot, doesn't it? But your rib cage alone, which protects your heart, is made up of about twenty-four separate bones.

In addition to the bones themselves, your skeleton also has a number of *joints.* Joints are the places where two bones meet. Most joints, such as your elbows and your knees, are movable. A thick, slippery fluid covers them so that they slide easily back and forth.

There are many types of movable joints. Ball-and-socket joints, such as the ones in your hips and shoulders, allow for free movement in a circle. Your elbows, knees, and fingers have hinge joints that allow the bones to move back and forth. A *ligament* is an important part of a joint. It is a tough band of slightly elastic tissue that holds the bone ends together. Ligaments make it more difficult for bones to come out of the joints or to break.

An illustration of the human skeleton, with the joints superimposed.

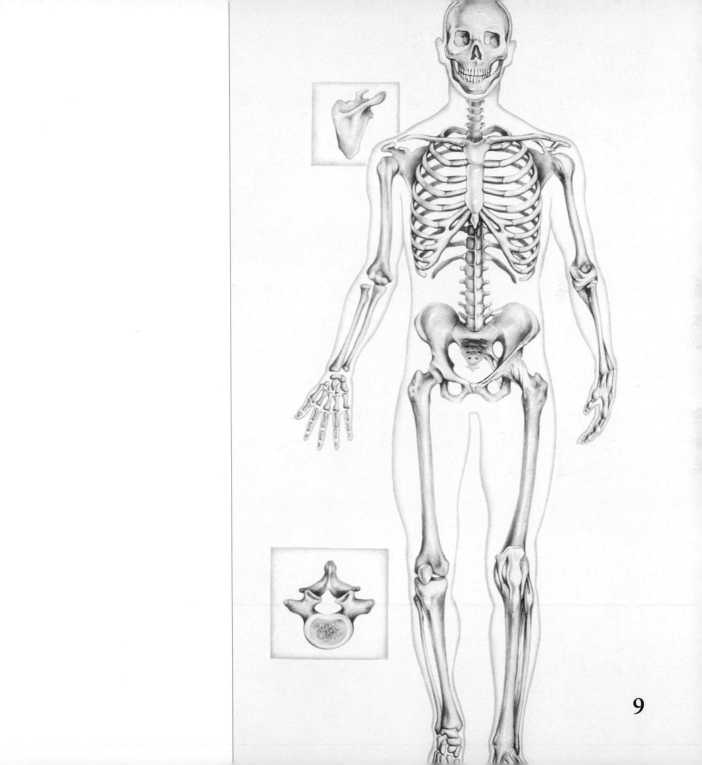

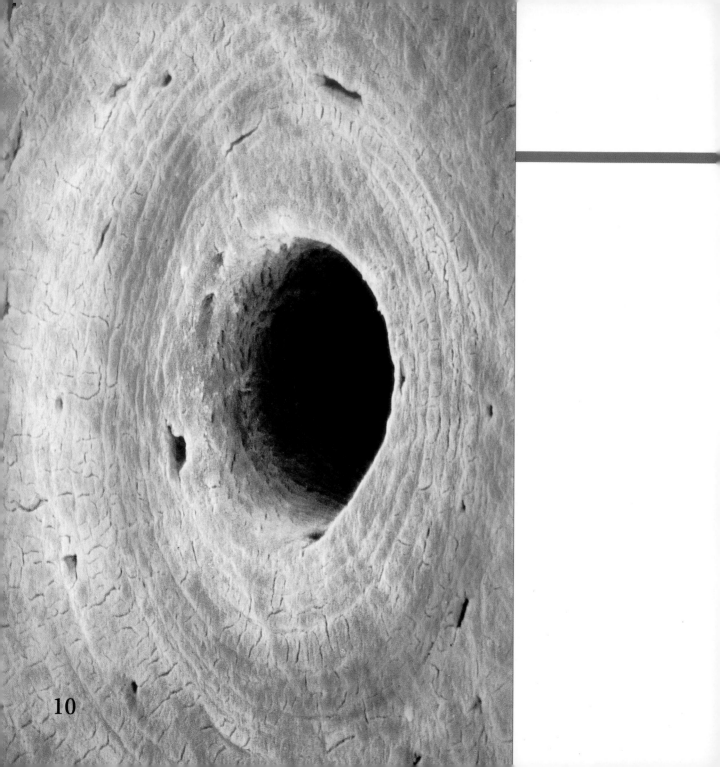

10

INSIDE YOUR BONES

If you were to take a living bone and cut it in half, you would see that it has many different layers. First, there is a layer of thin membrane packed with nerves and blood vessels. Next is a dense, rigid bone called the *compact bone*. The compact bone is shaped like a cylinder and is so hard that doctors must use a saw if they have to cut through it. The compact bone is filled with tiny holes and passageways that allow the nerves and blood vessels, hollow tubes that carry blood, to bring nerve messages and nutrients to the bone.

Compact bone is the densest, hardest layer of bone in the body.

11

The next layer inside the compact bone is called *spongy bone.* Spongy bone has many spaces and produces bone marrow. Yellow bone marrow stores fat and releases it when the body needs it. The body uses fat for energy. Red bone marrow makes blood cells in large amounts—red blood cells that carry oxygen and nutrients throughout your body and white blood cells to fight disease.

The bones are also storage places for minerals, particularly calcium, phosphate, and magnesium, which help make them hard. Bone tissue continually breaks down and rebuilds. In fact, about every seven years your body replaces what amounts to an entirely new skeleton.

Spongy bone is soft and filled with blood vessels.

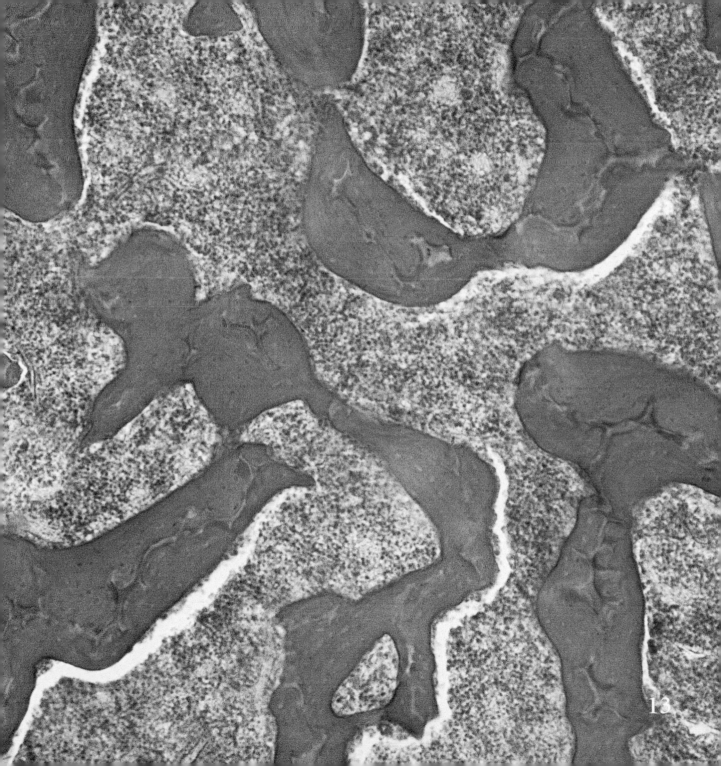

13

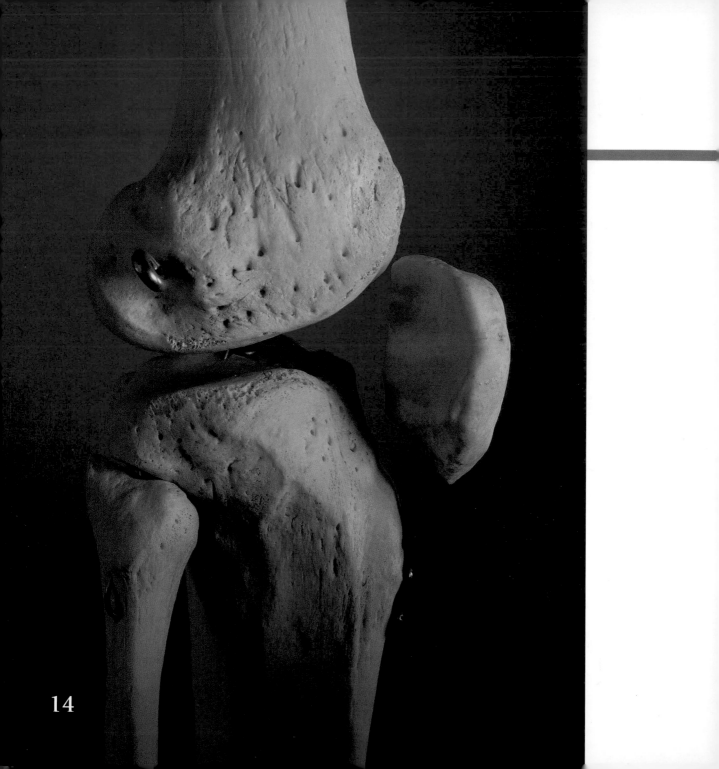

BONES FROM HEAD TO TOE

Did you know that the thighbone is the largest bone in your body? The *femur,* or thighbone, is the longest and heaviest bone in the body. It works with the muscles in your thighs and hips to help you walk and run. The knee joint, which connects the thighbone to the two bones of the lower leg, is the biggest and strongest single joint in the body. It has the ability to lock the leg in a straight line and bear the weight of your body when you stand and walk and run. It also bends so you can walk.

The knee joint allows your leg to bend so that you can walk. It is also strong enough to hold you up and bear the weight of your body.

Some of the smallest bones are in your feet and hands. Each foot and hand has twenty-six bones each, all of them small enough to allow a great deal of movement. Believe it or not, your skull has even more bones—about twenty-eight—but some of them fuse together during childhood to form wiggly lines called sutures. Eight bones form a protective box around the brain. Another fourteen bones give your face its unique shape.

Your skull, made up of twenty-eight bones, protects the soft, precious tissue of the brain. In this picture, the sutures are clearly visible.

16

17

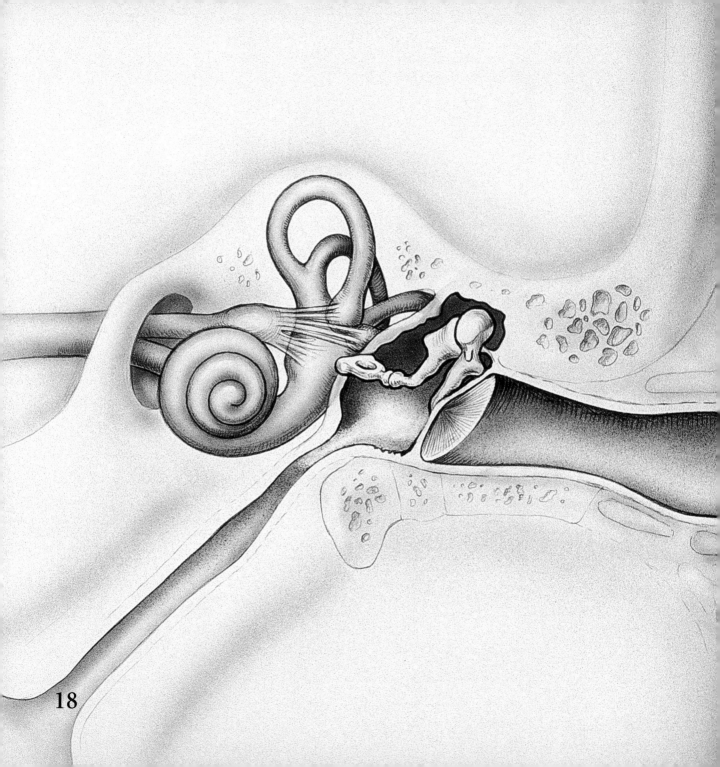

18

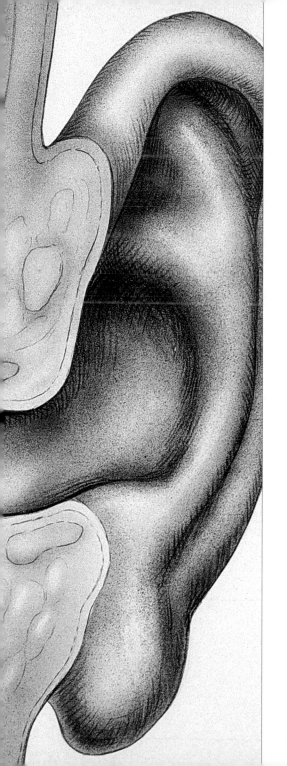

And the very smallest bones in your body are deep inside your ears. Each ear contains three tiny bones called *ossicles*, which help you hear.

The ossicles, the bones that help you hear, are the tiniest bones in the body.

Your spine, or backbone, is a flexible column of bones that runs down the middle of your back. It is made up of a chain of small bones called *vertebrae.* Joints connect the vertebrae together, and the structure of the whole column forms a flexible chain that can bend and twist.

Between the vertebrae are *disks,* which are like small circles of jelly between the bones. Did you know that you are slightly taller in the morning than you are when you go to bed? This is because the disks, which press together all day as you sit and stand, expand while you sleep.

The spine protects the nerve fibers that run from the brain to the rest of the body.

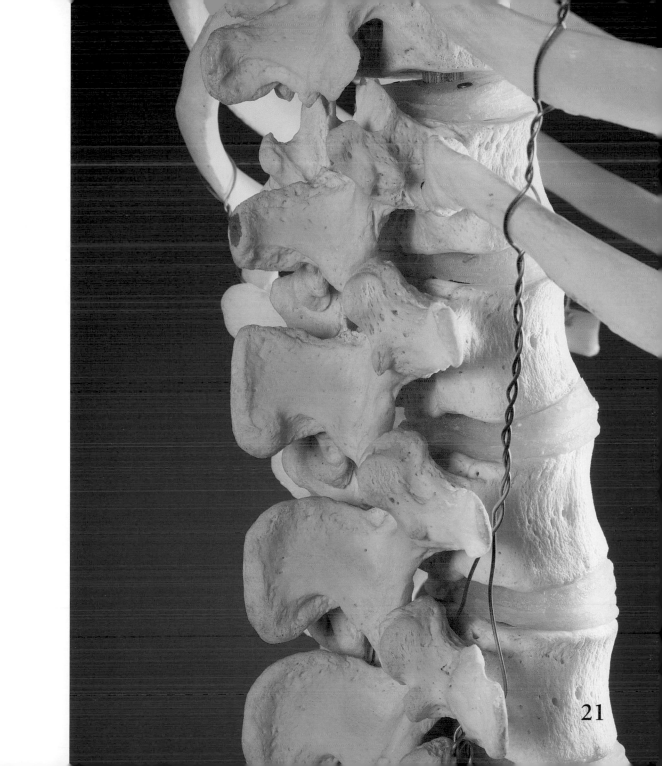

21

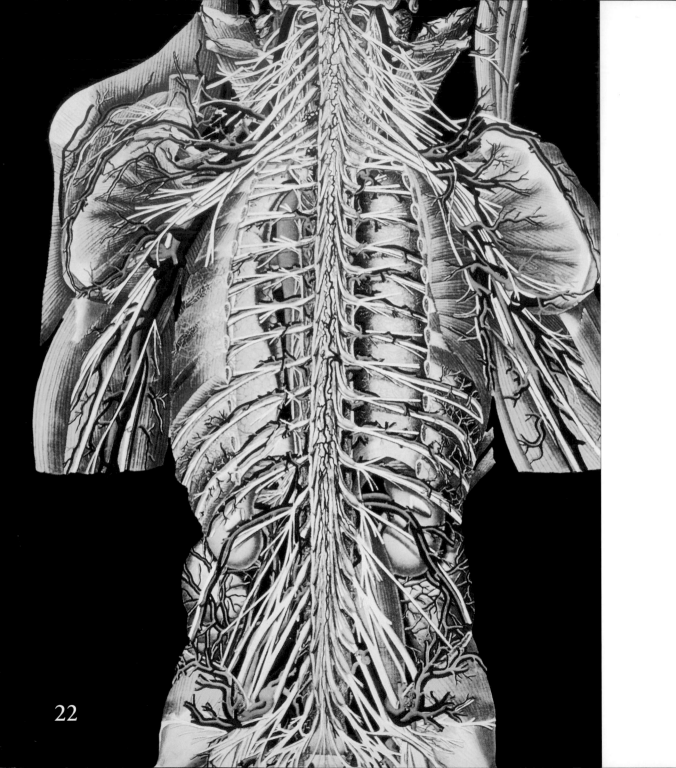

The *spinal cord,* a bundle of nerves, runs through the hollow of the vertebrae. Individual nerves come out of the spinal cord through the openings in the vertebrae. They transmit information back and forth between your brain and the rest of your body, including your muscles.

Nerve fibers that stem from the spinal column send messages to and from the body and brain.

MOVING WITH MUSCLES

As you read, the muscles that control your eyes move them across the page. Muscles in your arms, hands, and fingers let you hold the book steady. You also have to breathe, which uses muscles in your chest. Your heart muscle is working, too, to keep your heart beating. Your muscles are always moving, even while you sleep.

You have more than 650 individual muscles in your body. Muscles make up about 40 percent of a man's body weight and 23 percent of a woman's.

There are three kinds of muscles in the body. *Skeletal muscle* attaches to and moves your arms, legs, and other body parts. You have control over these muscles, which is why they are also called *voluntary muscles*. Most skeletal muscles are attached to bone or to other muscles by tough cords called *tendons*.

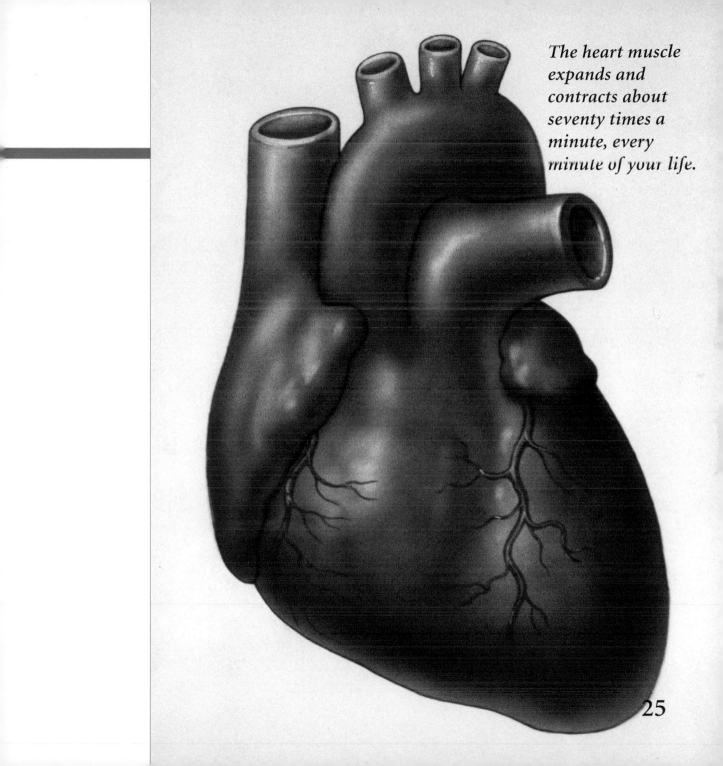

The heart muscle expands and contracts about seventy times a minute, every minute of your life.

25

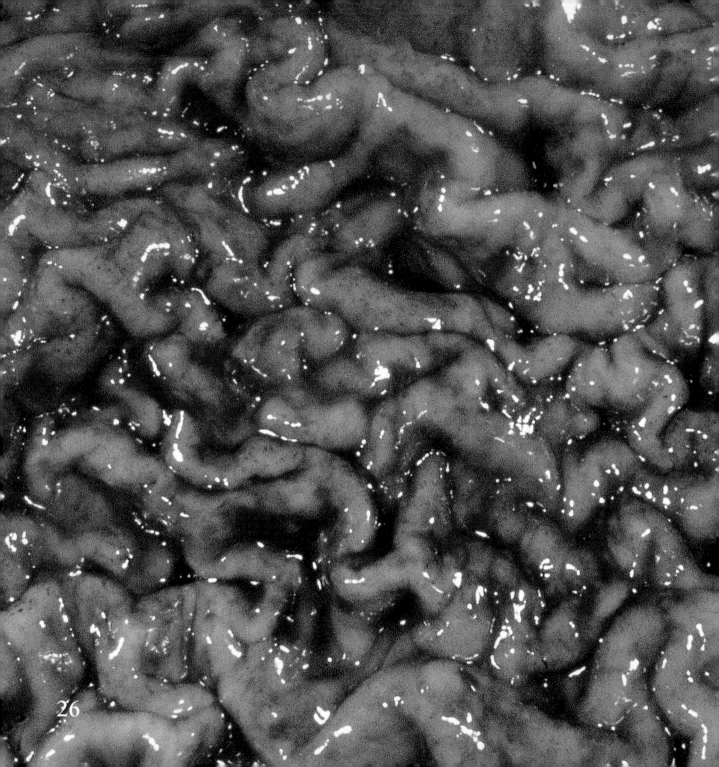

Another kind of muscle is called *smooth muscle*. Because you can't control smooth muscle activity, this type of muscle is also called *involuntary muscle*. Smooth muscle lines the walls of the stomach, intestines, and blood vessels, helping to push food along the digestive tract and the blood through the veins (vessels that carry blood from the body to the heart) and arteries (vessels that carry blood from the heart to the rest of the body.) The third kind of muscle, the *cardiac muscle,* controls the beating of the heart. Cardiac muscle continually contracts (becomes smaller) and relaxes (becomes larger), pumping blood around your body 60 to 70 times a minute, 100,000 times a day.

The involuntary muscles of your stomach help to move the food you eat through the digestive process.

HOW MUSCLES WORK

Picture a telephone cable: that's what the inside of a muscle looks like. Inside the cable is a bundle of smaller cables called *fibers,* and each of those bundles contains still smaller fibers called *fibrils.* In a long muscle, a single muscle fiber can be up to one foot long and as thin as a human hair. Fibrils are made up of two types of proteins: *actin* and *myosin.*

Many muscles are arranged in pairs, with each muscle in the pair performing an opposite movement. For example, when muscle fibrils in the leg receive a message from the brain to move, the actin strands slide past the myosin strands, which make the muscle contract. When the actin strands in your leg slide in the other direction, the muscle relaxes and your leg returns to its original position.

Muscle tissue is made up
of a bundle of cables
called fibers, which are
up to one foot long.

Your face contains many muscles that allow you to smile, frown, chew, and talk.

MUSCLES FROM HEAD TO TOE

Smile! Now think about how many muscles you used for that simple act. Your face and neck have more than thirty different sets of muscles. Most of them are small and are attached to each other rather than to bones. Certain muscles help you express your moods. You use two muscles to pull up the corners of your mouth when you want to smile. Two other muscles raise your eyebrows when you want to show that you are curious or surprised.

Some of your strongest muscles are those that control the movement of your mouth and jaws so that you can talk and eat. The muscles of the lips, together with the tongue and the vocal cords in your throat, produce the many movements and sounds you need for speech.

The middle part of your body, called the torso, contains layers of different muscles that help you move and allow you to breathe. Your upper back also contains powerful muscles that help you stay upright and move your arms and shoulders. Deep inside your torso is a muscle called the *diaphragm,* which moves up and down as you breathe.

The largest and strongest skeletal muscles in your body are in your legs. The strong calf muscles at the back of the lower leg help your foot bend forward and also help bend the knee. They are connected to the heel bone by the *Achilles tendon,* the strongest tendon in the body. The biggest muscle in the body is the *gluteus maximus* in the buttocks. It helps to flex the thighs.

The upper and lower back, along with the thighs, contain some of the largest and strongest muscles in the body.

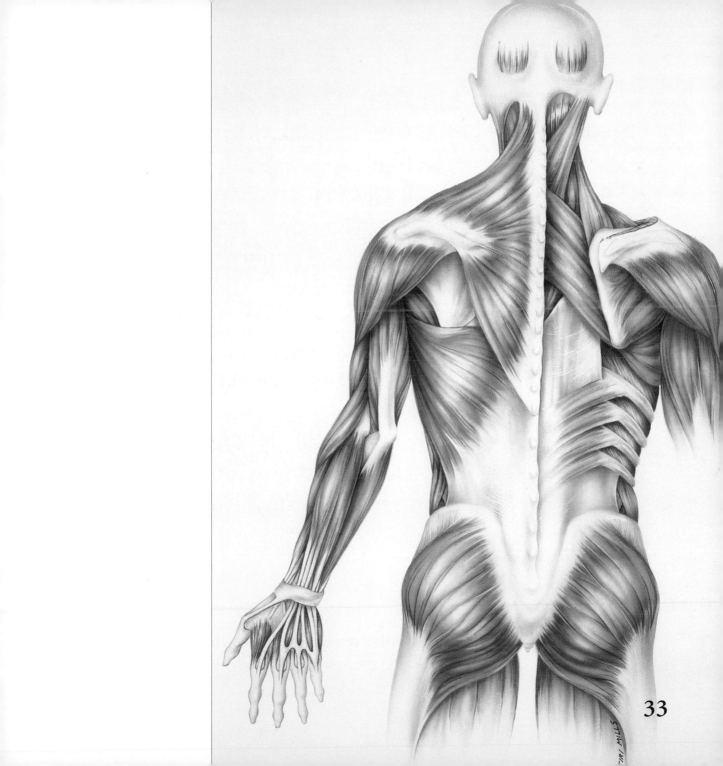

33

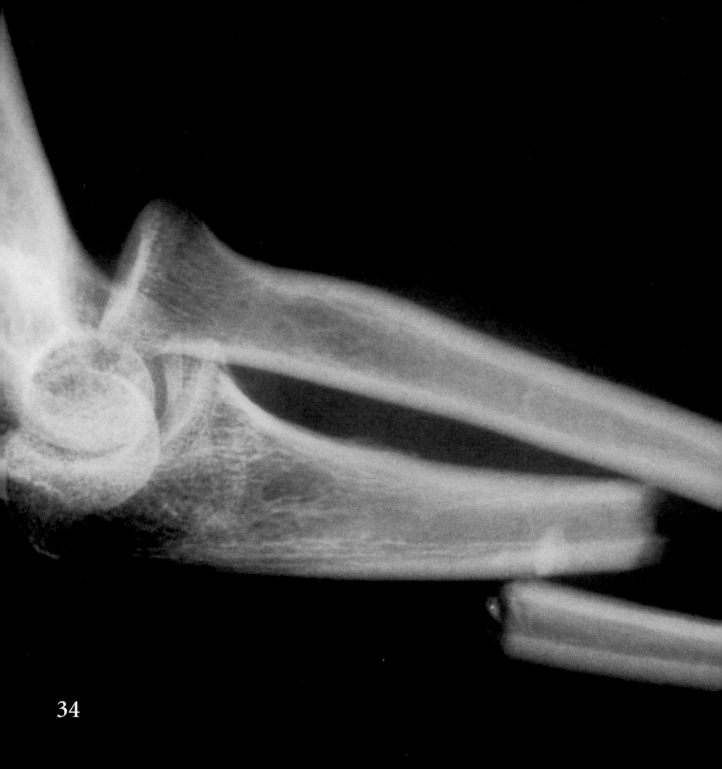

34

WHEN THINGS GO WRONG

Have you ever sprained your ankle or heard someone complain about his or her arthritis? If you're very lucky, you won't really have to think about the health of your bones and muscles. But there are some common conditions and injuries that can affect them.

Fractures

If you hit a bone very hard, or bend a joint too far in the wrong way, the bone will snap. A doctor will set a bone in a cast to keep it stable. A blood clot will form to close up the space between the broken ends, and the bone cells will grow on each side of the break until it heals.

As hard as bones are, they can break when enough force hits them. A fracture is the result.

Dislocations

When two bone ends shift out of the joint that connects them, it is called a dislocation. Often painful, a dislocation frequently also tears ligaments. Doctors treat dislocations by first putting the bones back into position and then keeping them stable for three to six weeks.

An X ray of a left hip showing a femur fracture with dislocation.

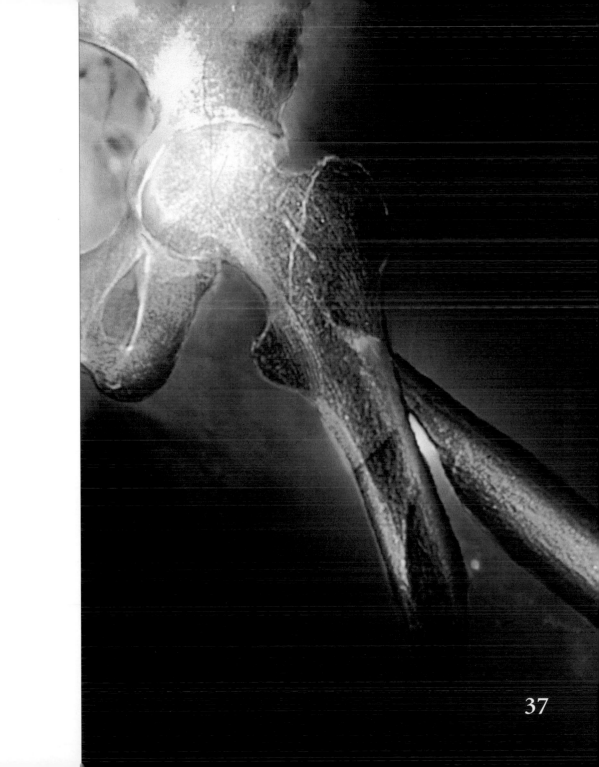

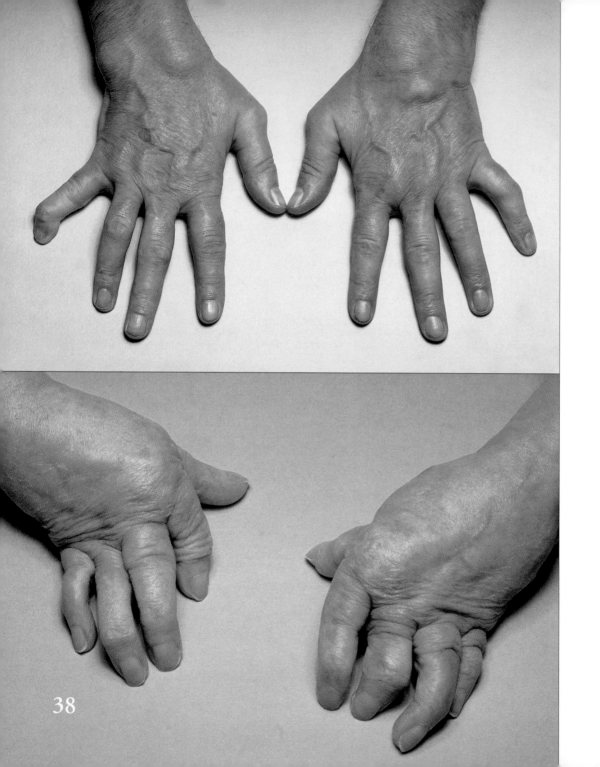

38

Arthritis

Arthritis is a group of diseases that causes joints to become inflamed and swollen. There are many different treatments for arthritis, depending on the type of disease and how serious it is. In very serious cases, doctors may replace the joint entirely with an artificial one.

Examples of arthritis and the disfigurement it can cause.

Muscle and tendon strains

Injuries to muscles and tendons are usually the result of using them too much and too hard during sports activities. Muscle strain occurs when muscle fibers are damaged. When muscles tear, they bleed, which can cause them to swell and bruise. Tendons may become inflamed when strong or repeated movement creates friction between the tendon's outer surface and a nearby bone.

If you twist your muscles or tendons too hard or in the wrong direction, you can cause them to tear. These injuries are known as strains or sprains.

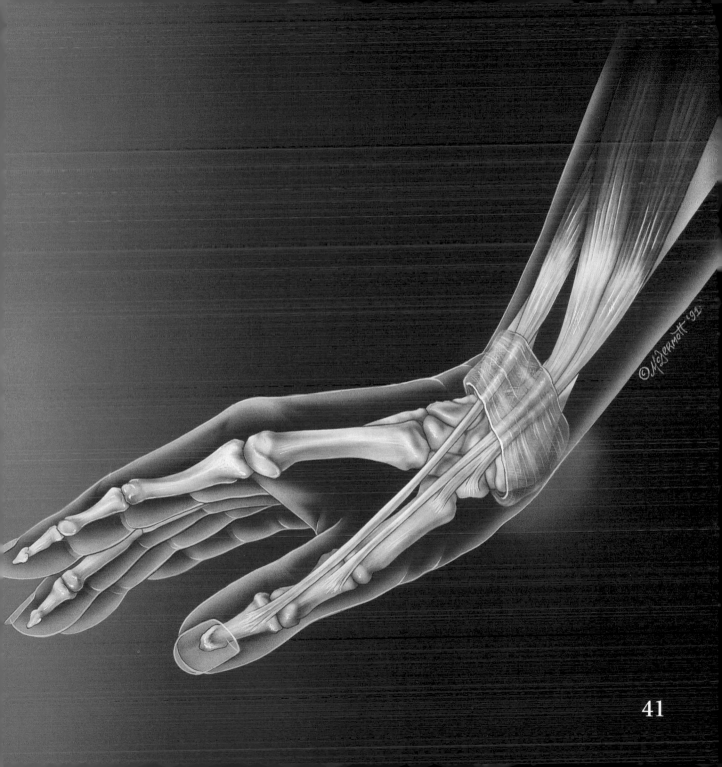

41

*Use them or lose them!
Exercise is the best—and
most fun—way to keep your
bones and muscles strong
throughtout your life.*

KEEPING YOUR BONES AND MUSCLES HEALTHY

If you eat a balanced diet rich in calcium—foods such as milk, yogurt, and spinach—you'll provide your bones with the minerals they need to build and rebuild themselves throughout your life. Exercise is most important when it comes to the health of your muscles. The more you exercise a muscle, the larger the muscle cells become. The blood vessels that enter the muscle widen so that the muscle receives more food and oxygen. Exercise doesn't create new muscle tissue, but it strengthens those you have. Without exercise, muscles shrink and tire easily. And they also become more easily injured. So if you want to stay up and running—make sure you eat well and get plenty of exercise!

GLOSSARY

Achilles tendon   a tendon that runs from the middle of the calf muscle to the heel. If the tendon is torn by injury, it becomes impossible to raise the heel

Actin   a protein that helps the muscle to contract, or draw together

Arteries   vessels that carry blood from the heart to the rest of the body

Cardiac muscle   the muscle that makes up the walls of the heart and allows it to contract and expand

Compact bone   a layer of bone tissue that is dense and rigid

Diaphragm   a muscle deep inside the torso that moves up and down as you breathe

Disk   a small circle of jelly between the bones of the vertebrae

Femur   also known as the thighbone, the femur is the largest bone in the body

Fiber   a tiny threadlike structure that helps to make up muscle tissue

Fibril   a very small fiber

Gluteus maximus   one of three paired muscles of the buttocks that work to move the thighs

Involuntary muscles   the muscles that are not under our control, including those of the heart and stomach. The brain directly triggers the movement of this type of muscle tissue.

Joint   the place where two bones meet

Ligament   a tough band of slightly elastic tissue that holds the bone ends of a joint together

Myosin   a protein in the muscles that help them to move

Ossicles   the smallest bones in the body are located in each ear and help in hearing.

Skeletal muscle   voluntary muscle that attaches to and moves your arms, legs and other parts of the body

Smooth muscle   involuntary muscle that is controlled directly by the brain, such as the stomach and intestines

Spinal cord   a bundle of nerves that runs through the hollow of the vertebrae

Spongy bone   a layer of bone responsible for producing bone marrow

Tendon   a strong band of fibers that joins muscle to bone

Vertebrae   the thirty-three bones that protect the spinal cord

Voluntary muscles   the muscles that you can move when you want, such as the muscles of your legs, arms and face.

FIND OUT MORE

BOOKS:

Clayman, Charles, ed. *The Human Body: An Illustrated Guide to Its Structure, Function, and Disorders.* London: Dorling Kindersley Limited, 1995.

Cumbaa, Stephen. *The Bones Book.* New York: Workman Publishing Company, 1992.

Llamas, Andreu. *Muscles and Bones.* Milwaukee, WI: Gareth Stevens, 1998.

Llewellyn, Claire. *The Big Book of Bones: An Introduction to Skeletons.* Peter Bedrick Books, 1998.

Parker, Steve. *Muscles.* Brookfield, CT: Copper Beech Books, 1997.

Sandeman, Anna. *The Children's Book of the Body.* Brookfield, CT: Cooper Beech Books, 1996.

Simon, Seymour. *Bones.* New York: William Morrow, 1998.

WEBSITES:

The Human Skeletal System
http://www.shockfamily.net/skeleton/

KidsHealth
http://www.kidshealth.org/kid/body/bones_SW.html

KidsHealth
http://www.kidshealth.org/kid/body/muscles_SW.html

AUTHOR'S BIO

Suzanne LeVert is a writer and editor of young adult and trade books with more than 30 titles to her credit. Although she specializes in health topics, Suzanne also enjoys writing about history and politics and is the author of *Louisiana* and *Massachusetts* in the Benchmark Books series, Celebrate the States. Suzanne currently lives in New Orleans, Louisiana, and attends Tulane Law School.

INDEX

Page numbers for illustrations are in boldface.

Achilles tendon, 32, 44

actin, 28, 44

arms, **5**

arteries, 27, 44

arthritis, **38**, 39

back muscles, 32, **33**

biceps, **5**

blood cells, 12

blood vessels, 11, **13**, 27, 43

bones

    largest, 15

    layers, 11–12

    number of, 7, 16

    rebuilding, 12

    smallest, **18**, 19

    uses, 4, 7, 16, 20

breathing, 32

buttocks, 32, 44

calcium, 12, 43

cardiac muscle, 44

childhood, 7, 16

compact bone, **10**, 11, 44

contraction, 28

diaphragm, 32, 44

digestive tract, **26**, 27

disks, 20, 44

dislocations, 36, **37**

ear, **18**, 19

eating, 31

energy, 12

exercise, **42**, 43

face, 16, **30**, 31

fat, 12

feet, 16

femur, 15, 44

fibers, 28, **29**, 44

fibrils, 28, 44

fractures, **34**, 35, **37**

fusion, 7, 16

gluteus maximus, 32, 44

hands, 16

health tips, **42**, 43

heart, **25**, 27

height, 20

joints, 8, **9**, 20, 45

    See also arthritis; dislocations

knee, **14**, 15

leg muscles, 32

ligaments, 8, 45

    See also dislocations

magnesium, 12

marrow, 12

minerals, 12, 43

moods, 31

movement, 8

muscles, **29**

    information transmission, 23,

    injuries, 40, **41**, 43

    largest and strongest, 32, **33**

    number, 24

    pairs, 28

    proteins, 28, 45

    skeletal, 24, 45|

    smooth (involuntary), **26**, 27, 45

    strengthening, 43

    uses, 24, 31, 32

    voluntary, 24, 45

    See also heart

myosin, 28, 45

nerves, 11, **22**, 23

nutrients, 12

ossicles, **18**, 19

oxygen, 12, 43

phosphate, 12

proteins, 28, 44, 45

rib cage, 7

skeleton, 4, 6, **9**, 12

skull, 16, **17**

spinal cord, **22**, 23, **23**, 45

spine, 20, **21**

spongy bone, 12, **13**, 45

strains, 40, **41**

sutures, 16

tendons, 24, 45

thighbone, 15, 44

veins, 27

vertebrae, 20, 23, 45